Piece O' Cake Desi

whimsic designs
coloring book #1

MW01157195

18 Fun Designs + See How Colors Play Together + Creative Ideas

LINDA
BECKY

Meet the Artists
Becky Goldsmith & Linda Jenkins

When Becky and Linda met, they knew they wanted to make quilts together, so they formed a company called Piece O' Cake Designs. Even when they moved to different places (Becky lives in Texas and Linda lives in Colorado), they continued making quilts together. They created the designs that are in this coloring book and use them on the quilts they make.

Playing with color makes them very happy. The world is full of beautiful colors and patterns that give them ideas and they love to use this inspiration in their quilts. They say "Feel free to doodle and draw new designs of your own. Use every color in the box! Have fun and be happy!"

Do You Know What a Quilt Is?

This coloring book and others in this series are based on designs and techniques for making quilts. A quilt is made of three layers: fabric on the back, fabric on the front, and a soft layer in the middle called batting. The three layers are held together with stitching, called quilting. Some quilts are made to be used on a bed. Some quilts hang on the wall as art.

Often the top of the quilt is made up of many pieces of fabric sewn together to form a pattern.

Becky and Linda use appliqué (a-plə-ˈkā) to make their designs. Appliqué is a style of making quilts where the design is made up of pieces of fabric that are cut out and sewn on to the top of the quilt. The pieces usually form a picture. You can see pictures of Becky and Linda's appliqué quilts to the right and on the back cover of this book. They are art quilts, meant to hang on the wall, rather than being used on a bed.

Quilters and artists often use color wheels to find good color combinations to use. Be sure to look inside the back cover for a color wheel that you can use to see how colors play together.

lollipops from *The Best-Ever Appliqué Sampler* from Piece O' Cake Designs